Freeflow Books
Copyright ©2017
ISBN: 978-1548279141
Library of Congress Catalog Card Number: "Library of Con-
gress" is an oxymoron. More like "Charnel House of Death's
Architects"

Cover design by Rose Throop

# Practicing Ordinary Life

by Ron Throop

*I was perplexed as to what the usefulness of any of the arts might be, with the possible exception of interior decoration. The most positive notion I could come up with was what I call the canary-in-the-coal-mine theory of the arts. This theory argues that artists are useful to society because they are so sensitive. They are supersensitive. They keel over like canaries in coal mines filled with poison gas, long before more robust types realize that any danger is there.*
— Kurt Vonnegut

Early morning woods walk with a friend. Unfortunately for him, he has hair, and the ticks leapt for it. He picked two off his scalp before noon. I secretly hoped to find one in a similar spot, but ticks are more sophisticated these days. They expect better quality for their risk investment. Not only are there fewer places to hide on my head than the day before, but ticks can sense a cynic. Always scratching his head. "Why? Why do it that way? Or any way for that matter?" Too much poking around on an already very thin area of follicle flora, and chance for engorgement is slim. Ticks know this. I am passed by for better coverage.

The woods were quiet. The world outside was getting busy. I think philosophers, as a job requirement, must spend a lot of thought-time seeking a path to contentment. All paths expect a destination, but few want to track one journey and end it there, living by its demands day in and day out unto death. Human life is never a market strategy, yet is often planned this way—as if the supreme judge is some stuffy bank president marking your application for the small business loan. On the last uphill climb of our walk my friend talked about a friend of his who, after being poor most of his life, has reached a point of economic security. Yet now he is persuading himself to go into another business for only he knows why. Just then the idea of the 6:00 p.m. peace popped in my mind. If you are at a point in life where enough money can be made, and no matter if you lose or win a little bit, a box of shredded wheat and rent is achievable, then count every success (both short and long-term) at the 6:00 p.m. marker (2nd and 3rd shift humanity can move the time to fit the individual situation). For instance, one wakes every day doing what is absolutely necessary to get to the after-dinner hour with total serenity. Food is digesting. Children are loved. Tomorrow is a long time. No worries to carry over to the morning. The appointment to have your teeth removed on Monday can always be canceled before 6:00 p.m. if you cannot stop thinking of your teeth being pulled out. The meeting at the institution needs assets you don't have because your daughter had a parasite in her stomach this morning... Then it is time to cancel any employment that demanded you give up your peace at 6:00 p.m. Union organizing didn't realize it a hundred years ago, but all it desired was the path toward the six o'clock in the evening wellness. Today, if poor people stopped trying to be poor people with smart phones, KFC counter work could very happily reward them with the 6:00 p.m. peace.

Success is subjective. To me failure is always an easy mark. Call anyone up a minute after 6:00 p.m. Oh, he answered? Ah-ha, you're both failures! But that's okay. See what you can do with tomorrow, such a very long time away.

Christmas must be a time to remember all the billionaires who swiped pension wealth back in 2008, and then fall down on our knees to the antichrist with the five boroughs accent, spewing fear and prejudice faster than the dependent puppies can lap it up. So many people love and admire scaredy-cat Donald Trump, it's no small wonder they haven't mobbed up yet and burned to a crisp anyone who doesn't look exactly like their mob in the mirror. The media has polarized our collective hope once again. If there are 30 people that think like Donald Trump, (not because they are told to by a television set, but truly gut-deep believe his every word), then the American Budweiser Biergarten Nazi party is reborn with several million servants who placate the spoiled brat because they get crime and punishment arousal from him.

I hate ignorance, which is the embodiment of our entire federal political process. Men and women candidates who don't even know what their job description entails. Demagogues, every one, selling hope like snake oil to a Kansas farm. Donald Trump and Bernie Sanders were selling hope, but the job each man was applying for was head of the executive branch of federal government. The latter enforces the laws made by Congress. It is supposed to be the boss of the military. It has its photo taken with boy scouts and it hosts state dinners. It cannot offer hate or love in the flesh. Trump then and now pitches the collective hope of bigots and life's losers, while Sanders placates the hope of dreamers and life's losers. A nation of 310 million picks its President from door-to-door salesmen, all information brought to the masses by a few billionaire media men, one an evil old Australian propagandist who is the spitting image of Joseph Goebbels and proud of it. That left-leaning New Yorkers have not flipped his limo in the street and dragged his rotting body to a solitary cell is proof of the nationwide ignorance I speak of.

We can't even call a thing what it is when we see it. Thinking on a subject for more than a few minutes is taboo. And, of course, because of light speed connection, everyone has an opinion. Even fools like me.

The mute majority are ignorant appeasers of institutional evil. That's most of us. The few good ones are like abolitionists who write and speak to crowds, but only one in 60 million is ever a John Brown.

Trump can give the country fear and hatred. Sanders, Clinton, as well as those half-lying to make a sell, can give it non-hate. But they are just President wannabes—not holy heaven-hell saviors. Presidents are good at suggesting bombing or "boots on the ground" in foreign lands of many brown people. They are very bad at "reality" as it is told to them by God knows who. Well, for a certainty, who ain't you and who ain't me, because both of us have read this far. That means we thought through a subject long enough to check the spelling. One or two mistakes maybe, especially in capitalization, but hell—we're not grammar geniuses. And we read a Constitution once or twice long ago, even though it wasn't mandated by the secret police. And better yet, we remembered part of it! That should count for something, right? The law of the land, three branches of government... Did wonders for that "peculiar institution" called slavery, yes?

The French Revolution and its Reign of Terror must have been quite a scrambling time for political elites. I will read up on it soon to get some safety precautions for the inevitable guillotine. It will be an easy read since I am not a power thirsty hooker of the human race.

Governor Rick Snyder of the state of Michigan is though, and he should be worrying his size 42 slacks off. His type A power psychosis sure had its hey day back when the peasants were quite happy being stupid, and took no offense at being labeled the "consumer class", because they were, and historically, poor people tend to agree with any label that works to cut a paycheck. But nobody in modern day Flint wants to consume lead water, even when their governor and the U.S. president force it down their throats on a gray Wednesday afternoon. The people know something is heavy metals in the state of Michigan, and they will become so much more unforgiving when their children forget how to dress themselves in the morning.

If I was the governor, I'd have a sympathetic cousin hide me out in his cabin up on Hubbard Lake in Northern Michigan. I would wear a wighat, call myself "Dick", and never ever talk to anyone. But then again, I am a peasant, and not an elitist power hooker. As far as I know I have not helped poison school childrenand lied about it. And if I did make a child sick, very sick, through my avoidance and negligence, I absolutely would never want a job that reminds me, day after miserable day, of my sick and twisted offenses to the human race.

Last week my family visited Hoover Dam. Wow. A do-nothing Depression President allowed for the greatest engineering marvel of his time to begin construction. Humans being human to each other, and fixing problems. The greatest dam of its time, enough concrete to stretch a highway from San Francisco to New York City, gigantic ice blocks used to set the winged figures of the republic into black dolerite, which, according to sculptor Oskar Hansen represented "the immutable calm of intellectual resolution, and the enormous power of trained physical strength, equally enthroned in placid triumph of scientific accomplishment."

Gotta love elaborative sculptors.

He also wrote that Hoover Dam was "a monument to collective genius exerting itself in community efforts around a common need or ideal."

80 years ago. Humans being human to humans. My father told me that when he was a boy, my grandfather spun him many engineering stories about the construction of the Hoover Dam. He went to Cornell in 1932 to study mechanical engineering. Professors and students probably spent hours and hours talking about the dam thing.

I am calling out the President of the United States. You are not even close to the level of a defeated Herbert Hoover. You are obviously a puppet who has no real power. Drinking a few ounces of lead water does not make you a good president. It makes you a very bad one. Certainly a weak one. A power hungry figurehead to our defeated republic.

Likewise, Governor Snyder, and anyone who supports him as a man who still wants to be governor, is the lowest of low, rock-bottom, of the criminal class. Our own governments have gone mafia to corporate power.

I made a painting of the governor's severed head sinking in the Flint River. I do not feel bad for this. I am amazed that it has not yet been stuck on a post on the Saginaw Street Bridge. I don't know how much more we the people can be beat down before we rise up.

I guess they must think that if we ingest enough lead, we'll forget our own names, let alone our fingers, and where to point them.

Dear Bernie Sanders,

There is something decomposing in the neo-fascist state. Donald Trump will become the next President® of Earth. Hillary Clinton just picked a man nobody knows for VP. Everybody knows
you Bernie; millions would run to the polls ecstatic for you, and
you caved in to the fear of your newly acquired power to support a
Clinton Dynasty during what you called an ongoing political revolution. A tiny fraction of the millions who registered Democrat®
will go to the polls for Clinton. Clearly, you must see this. I have
little doubt that some professional outside force influenced you to
endorse more of the same. The majority of your supporters wanted
a royal King Sanders to finish the New Deal. Yes, that was dumb.
Many progressives have no idea who their Congress-person® is.
Could be a gun-lickin', serial Christ sniffing, right-wing, pretend
religious, Confederate fear-monger who loves to flag sex with
a federal government that legislates cultural laws and military
spending. You know this. There is precedent. Ron Paul couldn't get
Congress® to change. He wanted liberty, yet instead got a bunch of
tea-partying chanting bigots on parade. By abdication, you have
turn-coated to send a giant wave of confusion down the ranks,
confusion to turn into anger, and then nationwide apathy. Everything is just more cuckoo after you Bernie Sanders. You think that
you can keep moral high ground with the knowledge that both
Republican® and Democratic® nominees will kill a whole lot of tan
and brown people when picked for the monster prize. Trump will
egg it on in the cities at home (das Vaterland Furher), and Clinton
will give Boeing a cluster bomb boost with more Middle Eastern
kid's body parts to practice with (business as usual). Both are

disgusting human beings. And you claim to support one of them. What, in the name of our future, does that make you? Politics as usual. Several thousands, maybe a million, will struggle to hold on tightly to morality through a three month stream of media brainwashing, and cast their vote for a Gary Johnson, Jill Stein, or even neighbor Fred or Freida next door, who never in their lifetimes had anyone killed, roughed up, tortured, imprisoned, harassed, nor even purposefully embarrassed. It will be enough boost for the electoral college to choose Trump. And it is because of you, the only candidate to have a positive rating in this entire election process of insanity.

You took the fear plan, Bernie, hook, line, and Lake Champlain sinker. You fell for it so twentieth century! Jeff Bezos and the CIA won. No Donald Trump ever! Well, here is a little truth. At least, as far as the law or government can tell: Trump has never killed anyone. Clinton has voted and promoted the death of about a million human beings. Is this the game we play now to pick our Kings and Queens? Who is qualified to kill more people, to drone more babies, to threaten the use of more nuclear weapons?

"No solution is off the table," says the Grand Pooh-bah leader of money. "We shall use any means necessary to end the world. God bless. Good night. Now where's my dinner?"

How presidential. Thank you for protection Mr. Dumb Billionaire (Trump), Ms. Killvote (Clinton), Mr. Pretend Jewish Man (Sanders).

Donald is an unloved dandy. Hillary is avarice incarnate. Bernie, you think you're a rabble-rouser from 1968. All the young people are going to change the world and not morph into vile careerists at the first new car smell opportunity.

After igniting a passion for cultural rebirth and national sanity, you went inside yourself like a tired and frightened old man.

Therefore, to all and sundry, and especially Bernie Sanders without the conscience devil perched on his shoulder, I want these things from a federal government that collects taxes:

Passenger trains, exceptional care for the elderly, a national health care system, Apple, Inc® burned to the ground, Keebler® imprisoned, Boeing® jettisoned to the moon; I want Netflix® to have a flaming stick inserted colonly, schools that teach the joy of living, and streets to be named after artists and writers.

I do not want the following things from a federal government that collects taxes:

100 interns per Congress-person°, any energy source that will blacken my kid's lung, or potentially have her cat bear a litter of six-legged kittens. I do not want a military larger than Canada's, an oil pipeline through Sioux territory, nor another Rupert Murdoch crotch rot Budweiser° commercial.

Every federal vote I make from now on will depend on a candidate of a very similar kindred spirit. It is not up to the powerless to change the world. That is a heavy burden to bear for people who by the very reason of not being powerful, will never find the strength to restructure a nation.

But you are, or were anyway. And then you stopped.

Oh well.

Write-ins from now on.

Or, I'll just run for Congress° myself.

I am sick of government/media propaganda. Now that both leading Presidential candidates have loosely talked about nuclear weapons and their use, which translates as threatening all of life with very real (not pretend iPhone) power, and therefore admitting to premeditated mass murder, I have taken the proverbial gloves off and challenged each to a thumb wrestle. I shall easily defeat teeny-fingered Trump, yet I still need to assess Clinton's viable opposable, which at last account was thirty inches into Kissinger, and threatening to tickle his duodenum...

It's time to come down hard on the people of this nation. All of the post-pubescent ones anyway. Those who believe that any politician anywhere takes on the Jesus problems that all mid-level spiritualists burden themselves with on an hourly basis. Politically, we, the dumb pick-up truck or hybrid car coolies of inertia, deserve exactly what we get since atrocious food supplements like Apple Jacks® first found their home on cereal shelves across America.

Donald Trump rises to presidential possibilities because people who pretend to be liberal or conservative in America are still allowed to procreate, and worse still, raise their offspring. As adults we repeat the stupidest run-on sentences sometimes. Such as, "I am all for no smoking in restaurants, but I think our government should make trade deals with China because Sam Walton cared a great deal for the less fortunate even if his bones should be dug up and ground into a dust and the dust smeared on the lips of a cross-dressing rear admiral who floats his greasy fat arse around all day and night on top of a nuclear warhead, ready to annihilate life because some dandruff-flaked old white or wanna be white colonial man ordered him to".

Phonies say stupid things like that all the time.

All the time.

How about this grammatically correct one? "Life is suffering". You would never know it from the way the Dalai Lama jet plane puddle jumps from one stage to the next. Like Mick Jagger dressed down with less obvious greed, but a similar desperate desire to be loved and relevant, and a subsidized private cook supper every night for the rest of his life.

Grow up! Or grow down, you freakin' phony clowns. Life is not suffering. Fortunate, healthy children don't suffer unless their parents hate them enough to pick a favorite for president.

Joe in North Carolina drives a truck for septic removal. His dad ain't a soft bigot like him, no; Joe senior is downright klu-kluxed— both of 'em wanna vote for President cause Trump's a New York City Billionaire. Makes sense to me, but never to 12 year-olds because America has reached this unprecedented stage of total adult degeneracy. This morning outside Wilmington, N.C. many, many houses are floating away because Trump is gonna pour America a great big Lake Agassiz while he flies in his mother's arse jumbo jet eight miles high, laugh, laugh, laughing at all the bloating and floating finger-lip gibberers who voted for him.

Whoosh! Whoa! A near miss in the sky. The Dalai Lama was escaping too, hightailin' it back to Lhasa where the oceans have not reached... yet.

Stop your snickering old Sanders and new Clinton supporters. Sure we have the collective power to stop the clouds from warming, or at best attach a giant vacuum hose into outer space and suck out carbon, while simultaneously feeding and educating everyone on earth and getting cheap insulin for the babies we stuff with poison-in-a-box brought to you by Business As Usual, Inc. God forbid we save ourselves from annihilation by enforcing the non-existence of nuclear weapon technology. We can't even legislate against plastic grocery bags! It would take a few screw drivers to dismantle thermonuclear death for all of earth's species. Screwdrivers! So, we're going to tax billionaires to halt global warming— nature's normal reaction to humanities' lust for the path of least resistance, which is exactly how floating water would behave if it could stuff its mouth all night long with pizza and wings from Dominoes®. Why not? Let's halt atmospheric warming with money. Always money! Fight global catastrophe with arbitrary coinage. What is money? It is metal and paper. It's earth, for crying out loud! Oh, I get it! We're gonna save earth with earth. As if earth gets no say in the matter. Brilliant lunatic/human logic.

All vanities are insane. However, the narcissistic baby boomers and their spawn need to be locked up now. Me and you. Right now. Children, cuff us. The baby-boomers got us into this mess and we (present-day, child-raising adults) have kept humanity bogged down in the slime, lapping up every last grocery like voracious bacteria.

Is there a solution in this rant, oh ranting Ron? Please hurry, we all have delusional promises to keep.

Yes, but unfortunately for humans, it's not a human one... Still, very acceptable among non-human populations. A human being wrote it out in picture poetry a generation or two ago. Here it is.

"O take heart, my brothers. Even now... with every leader & every resource & every strategy of every nation on Earth arrayed against Her—Even now, O even now, my brothers, Life is in no danger of losing the argument!—For after all .... (as will be shown) She has only to change the subject."
—Kenneth Patchen

Repeatedly, I suffer bouts of intense self-doubt that usually pres-
age a light epiphany of sorts. I get a new idea or a reaffirmation of
a past philosophy, and all is set back right with the world. Always
temporary though. Another self-doubt monster will invade my
psyche in due time. It never fails to torment again and again.

For some unknown reason, the life of my great grandfather
sprang into my mind this morning. Henry Throop lived in the
central New York area all his life. He was born in 1880, raised in
Lebanon, N.Y., attended Colgate Academy prep school, went to
Cornell to study civil engineering, married, and settled in Syracuse, where he worked as a railroad engineer, and then on his own
as independent engineer/contractor until his death in 1956.

I use his life often in writing and conversation to juxtapose
today's culture to the one of a hundred years ago. Was it a better
time? Who knows? I can say with certainty that Henry was a very
mature twenty-something year old. He kept a journal—observations and day to day experience for the most part, and also a
seperate expense account book, showing where every penny went.
Every single penny! This morning's idea was to use this account
book to revolutionize the way I intend to sell my work.

### My Silver Dollar Campaign

I have had it with business and art. It doesn't work. The moment
the painting gets offered, haggled, denied, etc, on the market exchange, the entire culture of the thing created gets violated. I lose
all semblance of its original innocence as soon as the money door
opens. Only once have I made a painting thinking about money,

or a sale. Here it is:

2014. Acrylic on canvas, 12 × 12"

I was invited to a rock concert with some friends where there would be a section of the parking lot cordoned off for vendors. I painted this the night before, and had it sold before we finished putting up the tent.

It is stated in my great grandfather's account book that on September 14, 1907, he purchased the following for one dollar:

2 loaves of bread
1 dozen cookies
toothpicks
paper
salt
chestnuts
peanuts
pound of butter
and a haircut...

A dollar in 1907 had the spending power of about $25 today,

without the haircut (some small luxury to prove how contemporary economists always seem to get it wrong). So, about $40 today would buy these goods Henry bought in 1907 for a dollar.

One dollar.

I love the silver dollar because it has an ever changing value on the money market. For several years I have watched its value move between about $15 to $35. And it's just a dollar! It also feels good in the hand, and I bet many of them in a small pouch attached to my belt (a lá Rimbaud), would feel even better.

Henry's items listed are worth any one of my paintings. No one is buying the luxury items I have made available. So I have sweetened the pot in order to avoid the money exchange problem for the rest of my life.

I will amass silver coins!

From this day forward, any one of my paintings not hanging in a gallery can be bought for a silver dollar. Not what a silver dollar will buy, but exactly one, shiny silver dollar. I don't want to barter anymore. I want to jingle coins in a pouch. I have set the value, and it is universal. Any size. Any painting not in a gallery. Of course, the buyer must pay for frame and also shipping on top of the silver dollar. I have some very big paintings. If they were purchased, I would have to charge a handling fee. (Quite a bit of work goes into hiring a tractor trailer to pick up at a residence). Frames, shipping and handling could be exchanged in paper currency, however, the painting itself—always just one silver dollar.

Please think about this, and spread the idea far and wide. There must be a painting of mine that someone likes for such a fair price. I am just so exhausted from these encounters with the self doubt monster. It's time to kill the money.

Think of unique gifts for birthdays and holidays. I look forward to jingling real silver coins in a pouch.

Politically, my countrymen adamantly hover atop the cracks in the facade. There is less of a superpower here than a loony one with big stupid guns. Culture however, has already fallen, and visibly smashed itself on the ground floor. Arrogant ignoramuses scorn intellectualism, artists are reduced to begging their neighbors, poets have perfected writing on every emotion besides "hate for a change", where an overall live and let live philosophy has warped into a "I am so afraid of you that my eyes hurt" kind of fear that has everyone scuttling back to their shelters like terrified crumb stuffed-cheek grubbing chipmunks.

My country of mind-disabled men and women is mostly an unhappy place of unbearably disgusting one-upmanship.

Which is a shame since Noam Chomsky continues to declare this United States the freest place to live on earth.

Noam lives inside his own sticky bubble. One tends to lean cognitively dissonant when a highly endowed university supports your genius forever. Yes, we are free, *to conform*. We are free to say mean things about plutocrats or welfare recipients. A man here is both toddler and doting parents to himself, put on the couch each night, his free speech zone, to marvel at dross and yearn for longer life without living. The plumber is free to read a book on psychology, to instruct his children on mathematics, to wine and dine romantic love until the end of his time, but he will attempt none of these things until Hollywood or *The New York Times* or the NRA tells him that now it is time to think about the joy of living beyond his next purchase.

And that time never comes. Philosophy is the weaker enemy of propaganda. And propaganda, like the U.S. military, never had any intention, post WWII, of picking on anything its own size.

July 4 is Independence Day. Read the Declaration of Independence. Obviously not such an oppressive government lover, that wily Tom Jefferson. Tough words from a guy who enslaved women to have sex with them, and later helped ratify a constitution that declared Tom legally righteous to be making it with a mere three-fourths of a person.

Still, slave master and bigot Tom, as leader of a nation, could easily fit a Hillary Clinton/Donald Trump morality beneath his dirty pinkie nail. Moderns cannot seem to understand, Hillary Clinton hasn't any slaves, but she (and her husband) have killed many politically incorrect, innocent brown children, and Donald Trump enslaves cheap labor around the globe in order to construct more triglycerides about his midriff—both have no existential problem with the existence of Fruity Pebbles® or nuclear missiles, and both are truly disgusting human beings.

Read the Declaration of Independence, and think on why Americans have no intention of taking on a corrupt government ever again.

My take on the reason for communal mass cowardice? A majority of people (always myself included) are getting paid. Pringles® still line precious supermarket shelf space, and all Americans have allowed themselves reduced to three-fourths of a person or less. However, trumping these depressing observations, is the sad truth that most are about as deeply curious for their children's future as pickles on ketchup smeared hot dog plates.

Today I will Achieve two  of the five Pillars of Islam in defiance of the goons in Washington.

I certainly can't make it to Mecca. Nor, do I think I would ever go into a country more brutal and cowardly than Saudi Arabia, for private reasons. But I will handle the other four, in solidarity with all of Islam. It's easy. Centuries ago, elders made it easy—just declare there is only one God whose name begins with "A", and you and your starving family won't be taxed by the bosses. Boy, I wish it was that easy today! Praise Allah, and no pennies get extorted from me to fund big bombs and battleships? Bring him on! I can always say we'll take that trip to the holy town, tomorrow, or the next day...

You can convert today too. Cat Stevens did it, and he was just another spoiled rotten rock and roller. Here's how:

Shahadah: sincerely reciting the Muslim profession of faith.

Salat: performing ritual prayers in the proper way five times each day.

Zakat: paying an alms (or charity) tax to benefit the poor and the needy.

Sawm: fasting during the month of Ramadan.

Hajj: pilgrimage to Mecca.

A few footnotes:

• Luckily there are no judges besides Allah on that sincerity pledge.

• I do not make any money today or tomorrow to give alms, so consider this post my charity (which is 100% of my labor)

•You don't really fast the whole month. Just no food or sex

during the daylight hours. Also, Ramadan could be more than
a half year away, so many day trips into Islam costs you one less
pillar.

•And once again, there's always tomorrow to enter crazy cake
Arabia.

So for today I am a Muslim. Tomorrow I will return to my
perpetual state of American confusion which I inherited from the
last generation. We got so smart during the 20th century that we
let religion fall by the wayside. Somewhere along Doubter Road
we began to relinquish belief and fear in a higher power over to
belief and fear in the human abstract power, like presidents and
military police. Even religion and university living became hollow.
Christian ministers and priests started to pray to their military
leaders and vice-versa. While I attended college in my youth,
a local sorority hung a banner above their door that read *Nuke
Iraq*. Surface ideas and fear gut reactions became the culture and
the culture became ca-ca. Today self-glorifying smart people all
over the land are mocking the litmus tests in the fake culture war.
Unfortunately, I need them to preserve my sanity. One test that always makes me a good Muslim in spirit (Good Christian too, and
Jew, Buddhist, Vedic reader and Zoroastrian): witnessing a 12 year
old child whom you love get visually molested my a Nicki Minaj
music video, and feeling mad. Really mad. Like "going religious"
mad. Maybe I'm old-fashioned, but I would rather be an orthodox
Somalian Muslim than an overworked, unimaginative somnam-
bulistic American idiot who ignores celebrity sex brainwashing
of his children. It's real. It's everywhere. It's happening now. It's
allowed. It is our culture. Yuck!

Both Nicki Minaj and Donald Trump are not anomalies. Both
are very prominent American personalities that we let happen
because our parents spoiled us rotten and went to sleep making a
living while keeping up with the Jone's. Likewise the myopic Jones'
thought nothing about the world beyond how it immediately
affected the Jones' personal wealth and success.

And, admit it, all of us despise the Jones'.

Live and let live philosophy (which is no philosophy at all. Rather a scaredy-cat reaction to what confuses irreligious folks like us),
has imbibed in Americans the loathsome Fox TV fear-religion expressed by a stupid Donald Trump. Likewise, historically, the same

must be said about all presidents of the past. Franklin Roosevelt imprisoned Americans at concentration camps like Manzanar— He did it with a snooty Harvard accent, which soothed the public confusion like a tonic. Your parents and grandparents were also fearful little wussies like Trump and FDR. I live near the Safe Haven Museum, hallowed ground of the concentration camp where anti-Semite FDR, via the persuasion of his wife Eleanor, finally allowed a ship of European (mostly Jewish) refugees to settle near the end of World War II. Why didn't she divorce the warmongering xenophobic husband of supreme intolerance? Because she lived and let lived! It was the popular idea in 1942 to round up innocent kids, steal their parent's homes, and lock whole Japanese families up in friendly desert prisons. Oh yes, and then annihilate some of their distant relatives with terrorist atomic weapons that were detonated by order of the next xenophobic and racist president, Harry Truman.

Come to think of it. Donald Trump is a legacy, not an anomaly.

But this does not make him more or less disgusting than any President of the past who assumed that his position in life gave him the power to rule over any man or woman. Scaredy-cats do that.

Join me and become Muslim for a day. Or, if you're a really brave American middle class agent of continuous xenophobia, stop paying federal income tax. Or break something federal that equals the tax you pay. Disenfranchisement is just that. Ask whole populations from the 19th and 20th century American south (and north). You cannot vote disenfranchisement away. You have to suffer. I don't want to be a Muslim, but I will suffer this one day in solidarity with those people who are still grossed out by a Niki Minaj, and those too who are irrationally fearful of a coward bully with a 3rd grade vocabulary. Who can say I am disingenuous? Only Allah.

And he knows all the fakers—both Muslim and infidel.

I had a sudden revelation and insight while baking chocolate chip cookies for an exhibition.

And that is this... I am a dog.

Picasso is a lion. But I am a dog. Picasso is dead. I am living. Thoreau wrote that "a living dog is better than a dead lion". As a living dog, I work harder than the now very dead lion Picasso—that is, I work in many more directions with octopus arms with results that he could not transpire cubistically onto canvas with one measly arm. I think he would agree. My cookies are excellent. Probably even better than his loving wife could whip up on a Tuesday night for both Paloma in the moment and Pablo to freeze for an upcoming November exhibition in Florence. Genius can become fanatical in purpose, like Picasso, but it damn well better be able to spot a finer spirit whenever it comes along. A finer whole spirit. Human is human. Art is art. In order for wee painters to sink the Titanic of art avarice into the cold gray sea, the sensitive ones among us must shout out "Dog!" to Picasso, and all of the silly overrated takers who infected the twentieth century and beyond with acceptance of manufactured celebrity.

Look here, I've been playing this show and tell game full time for nearly ten years. I know of many equal artistically dedicated painters who could claim the same, and much more in paint, but each would have to answer to him or herself if the whole person remains in tact and fruitful. Hindsight is 20/20. Now that the biographers have revealed so much about his surface life, I can declare that Picasso was nothing more than a living dog who painted. And if he never made claim to getting whacked by nirvana, then I am a better dog who paints, because I am alive making myself lion, and fully aware of it. This goes equally well to all others who are painting and struggling with like mind and octopus arms. We are virtually everywhere. Quick! Look behind you!

Ignore the present day movers and shakers. The MoMA P.S.1 is poison. Avoid it. We should not trust a non-artist to curate its art. One limo after another arriving to the gala. Millionaires without even one arm painting. In any artist's mind, the director of MoMA P.S. 1 is a living dog who does nothing for his world, no matter how big or small, besides hoard bones of personal status and comfort. There are only so many hours in a day to become that special. Too much power. Too much control over some enormity (such as the world's living art and artists), is no man's ability. Not even superman could carry that weight.

I rode in a limo once. My high school buddy Scott Nicotera won a radio station contest to go see *The Temptations* play in Saratoga—about 70 miles from our hometown. We sat with two DJ's and talked about music the whole time. I poured myself a scotch from the dry bar. It was warm and made me almost sick to drink, but I downed it anyway, because I didn't want to lose face in a situation where I had no training, and therefore, any right to be in. I got through the scotch and the night, but even at eighteen, realized that being a full-time phony was no way to run a life. And some time not too long after, I felt the stubs of future octopus arms protruding. I vowed never to release the phony in me, not for pay anyway, and instead use my many arms to create the richest life possible with the limitations afforded me. So far, so good.

Because Picasso knew me in a future like I know him in a past, he would agree that your $10 suggested entry fee to MoMA P.S. 1, to see the games that a rich German snob thinks superb, would better behoove you and all of life to spend it instead on a local masterpiece, of your own choosing. Also, I am sure Picasso wouldn't know what the hell is going on lately with all this conceptual theater being performed in art galleries. Yea, it's clever, but a good one-armed painter could conceptualize the best of it with fingernail effort, and also give you paintings to look at for Pete's sake!

I say humility and personality must come through hard copy

in art in order for the once living dog (now dead lion) Picasso,
and the present living dog (most likely not to become dead lion),
Throop, would want to see before purchasing and bringing into
our homes, to share with people whom we love.

"McKay's Bunting Thinks People Do What They Are Told To Do"
2016. Acrylic on canvas, 20 × 24"

McKay's Bunting summers on St. Lawrence Island in the Bering Sea. He thinks the human fauna of the two mainlands (Russia and the U.S. are crazy to put up another second with big city lawyers and mafia goons manipulating an arbitrary system to their own ends. He believes localism is the answer, that human communities of all sizes should adapt to similar versions of the Golden Rule. He has graciously offered the peoples of the world a warm guano perch to imprison the present-day chiefs of oppression, and also the acting presidents of both human geographies which his tiny eyes can spy from hard rock hill.

However, this bird is not that naive. He is well read in late 20th century psychology, and knows the works of Solomon Asch and Stanley Milgram. When the people are ignoramuses, they provide themselves two choices for king of the human beings. When the people are stupid and afraid of their own children, they do this over and over again. Bunting watched a film once about Milgram's experiments at Yale. Humans "electrocuted" other humans for no reason other than they were told to by a stern human dressed up as a McKay's Bunting. It was surreal, and sent him into a deep depression, enough to scorn all mating ritual the following spring.

Thankfully, he's over that crippling condition now. A couple summers on St. Lawrence Island, and this sexy she-bunting giving him the eye, has cured him of the human psychosis. He's glad that birds aren't stupid. He is thankful for oceans of fish and rocks with wind. The humans can go rot, he thinks. Bunch of whimpering insects! Phooey!

My gut feeling (which is often art) tells me day after day that many, maybe even most, college and university art professors are not artists themselves, although they craft pictures or sculptures from time to time. They are more like  ministers of obsolete dogma in a practically defunct religion, like radio preachers, pretending a common and lazy vogue Christianity to make a living. I would feel sorry for them if so many weren't so damn arrogant.

But is it truly arrogance?

I guess not. Though sometimes their mannerisms come off that way. Can creative people even be arrogant? We are often self-loathing, sure, which breeds a tendency to be catty in some social situations. I used to think that my local college art professors stayed away from my painting exhibitions because they were arrogant. Yet lately, after much thought about it, I believe it's carefulness born from avarice which goads them to ignore my invitations. And "carefulness born from avarice" can hardly make "new" or "inspiring" art. One thing I know for sure. Art should bring people together. Therefore college art professors who do not exhibit to the community are not artists, per se, but rather, as any institutional job description would verify, *players of art*. They get paid to teach, some even by example. They may make wonderful images, sculpt beauty, perhaps manipulate digital media with the same attention medieval monks manuscripted. But these makers of things cannot be artists until they bring people together. Not by the force of college tuition, but rather through the playful and painful expression of their own intuition.

In my small city we have an art guild renamed an association some time ago. It is supported through yearly memberships and a rent-free grant from the mayor and city council.  Each spring for the past twenty years it has hosted a juried exhibition open to entries from anyone living in New York State over 18 years of age, provided he or she thinks the art worth a $20 entry fee, which buys a yearly membership. There are perhaps 30 fine and digital art professors employed at the college. Oftentimes the juror is selected from this learned group—most are credentialed with terminal degrees earned in their mid to late twenties. The juror gets paid a modest stipend, judges the work to be entered, 1st, 2nd, 3rd, Best in Show, and up to five Honorable Mentions, all receiving a small cash award, peaking at $300 for Best of Show.

Rarely do these professors submit their own work to be judged, though it is encouraged by the association. Several give direction to their students to apply.

Now why is that?

Because few of them are artists.

Anyone can make art—kids, students, moms, dads, celebrities, even cats I hear. But artists should bring people together. Even if it's just a group of other image-makers in a barroom or a poker game. The writer in isolation can make art if the work completed gives meaning in expression to other human beings. But if he doesn't get out once in a while with other expressive writers to be human among them, then nada as an artist. Art should bring people together.

I know from the grapevine that many of these professors apply for grants and/or exhibition opportunities from international institutions, in order to build resume and chalk up apparently concrete accolades from the most abstract and subjective of endeavors. If art success looks good on paper, a better retirement package ensues. A big thing among art teachers these days is to "go on residency", and those applications want "professional" credentials listed, and a several page C.V. (stands for "correctly vetted"), because institutions cannot judge originality and meaning in expression—only individual people(s) can do that. I think the university stifles originality across all disciplines. It is especially debilitating when it turns sensitive, creative people (new art professors) into ladder-climbing automatons. This distortion of art and art principle gets passed down to pupils. And then a vicious circle.

But on a personal note... How dare these professors send their students to have work judged locally, and yet not join the same game out of mutual respect!

And yet, I still do not think it is born from arrogance.

Perhaps fear.

What if one of these students won Best in Show? How would that reflect on the professor's residency application? I say very well if said professor was applying for a residency in the art and practice of pedagogy.

Another point. Art professors are not artists until they show their art at every possible opportunity. Especially locally. My goodness, where do these people think they live? Vienna? Paris? A 3-month long prestigious art retreat in Appalachia?

No. They buy eggs at the same convenience store I do. And for the record, I also send exhibition invites to the convenience store cashiers, yet they never attend. Maybe they graduated from art school, who knows? I expect those people who teach art to support image-makers outside the institution who help secure art teaching jobs jobs into the next generation. Artists make the art history of the future. We bring people together. We show paintings to the local clan. In any Neolithic community I'd be considered one of the clan artists. Those making private cave drawings to be seen first by elders of other clans from far away would be shunned like bad medicine, or maybe even banished from the clan.

I want to make it clear to the art faculty at my local college. Shame on you! When we cold share a beer, listen to some music, discuss art and artifice like human beings gathered together at local exhibition parties, very few of you are anywhere to be seen. Off building resumes that nobody gives a damn about. Some students are exhibiting their work at the art association, and painters like me will be there too. I hope your pupils can detect the irony of your absence, and vow to take a path less traveled by, to become artists themselves one day. I believe college art professors have the power to make revolutionary change to the face of any modern art. For god's sake, you all have summer's off and can afford materials! Do you truly believe there's a single clan in Melbourne or Prague that wants to see anything *you* make? *Their* local institution might pretend to, but the people sense that the institution, like the university, is a very broken construct. Much art is created in universities and exhibited at institutions, but very few artists are ever made there.

I made a painting fast and slapdash the morning after the 2016 Presidential election. I didn't care about the result, yet still felt a little queasy, and I knew why. The previous week three little birds got into my bowels and flew about. I wrote the following during their initial entry:

Very early yesterday morning I went to the grocery store, like I do most Sundays, to avoid the weekend rush of harried afternoon shopping. Lately, I have been planning ahead dinner meals for the coming week to get all ingredients in one shot. I used to be a daily market visitor until I realized that I hated our supermarket, because it was making me enormously depressed—not good when cooking occupies a large chunk of my day. I have sought liberation and wisdom my whole adult life, and several hours a day cooking for children and wife, makes musing a regularity. More than a thousand life changes, both real and imagined, have been contemplated in the kitchen—Philosophy, for me, began when I got a hold of *Nature, Man, and Woman*, by Alan Watts, and during the same season, realized that a fabulous soup can be made with cheap, wholesome ingredients.

Picking up rice in aisle three I overheard three men my age talking about the virtues of bottled marinade sauce. All agreed that the Olive Garden® brand was best. Of course, it isn't, and I use the term "men" strictly in its biological sense. What would have been best for supper was if Zeus sent a blazing hot thunderbolt onto their processed conversation, charring them good and proper for Polyphemus the cyclops to devour with sea salt and olive oil.

These men were life-haters—non-appreciative, non-nurturing, non-dreaming, self-entitled voracious consumers of anything under the sun that their economic class could afford them. In a phrase, ignorant emperor sloths. To each there is no one wiser, no teacher, no greatness beyond a wife who puts up with his diarrhea moanings from the bathroom after a night of beer drinking and slurping a soup of Olive Garden® marinade. Just as soon as the cramping is gone, however, the wife loses her status, and the ignorant emperor sloth is free to pretend all over again that his opinion matters, that diversity is a conspiracy to impoverish Caucasians, that guns don't kill people, that because it snows in January, global warming is a monumental, liberal hoax.

All economic classes are caught up in illusions so thick, that they also share important opinions on marinade sauce. Once in a while the topic turns to saving the world one savior candidate at a time. But each still wants what the other one wants. That is, to have everything on a straight path without stumbling, and the bliss of ignorance, to cover up the gnawing despair which a linear path reveals. So, they discuss the virtue and vice of a Hillary Clinton, or Donald Trump, when one is a killer and the other a pervert. Even the smartest book-smarters don't see that a people gets the government it deserves. The media did not make these two cowards of the human race. Sure, it's responsible for Olive Garden® marinade, but it's the individual, you and me fat Charlie, who ate the world and now complain about stomach cramps.

I too am an ignorant emperor sloth. I think on it every day. I began thinking it 25 years ago while spooning the oatmeal into my toddler's mouth. The ignorance and arrogance consummation of modern man has reached its climax. I only visit aisle three for my rice and beans, and occasionally a can of chipotle peppers when the feeling arises. You want to talk about choice marinades while your children watch Presidential candidates® practically have rough sex on an international stage? Go for it, since you(we) already do, every day, while obtaining choice stuff under the sun, and then blaming the other guy for it.

I made four paintings in as many days. During these creative hours I noticed worldly adult men, maybe women, but I only see men, playing apocalypse games with my life and destiny. So I decided to write about figuratively wrapping my fingers around their windpipes and squeezing until all heads pop off. Using my dream arsenal to fight fire with fire must work, else old, dying men like John McCain and Benjamin Netan-YaHoo win, and all hopeful children of earth, lose big time. Netan-YaHoo. I stress the last two syllables in the name of the Israeli prime minister to remind readers that we are dealing with pure Confederate flag waving segregationist, and Apartheid-loving evil. He is a yahoo. A pretend Jewish yahoo. He is Jewish like Ghandi was Hindu if being devout meant smiting all people not Hindu with sophisticated weaponry purchased from the British. Pretend prime minister Netan-YaHoo is propped up by a U.S. tax paying pretend citizenry. The latter are burdened with a media of which it seems that no published member has yet taken a civics course in his or her (but mostly his) lifetime. A yellow corporate journalism that is bought and paid for by who knows who—certainly not by poor painters, nor Oklahoma and Wisconsin bigots who voted a vile and corrupt New York City billionaire to the presidency. The unconnected citizenry (99.99%) have no clue who runs Earth, Inc., though so many of them often pretend to know the geopolitical strings that are pulled and state their opinions freely using the yellow journalists bought-and-paid for points of argument.

Because real political information does not flow to the masses, unless provided by an Edward Snowden or "Russian" hackers, or god forbid, a personal drive to acquire a sense of history beyond what the *New York Times*® wrote was real last night at 7 p.m.—

Because all of us, yes, even unsophisticated yet overly opinion-ated Ron Throop, have no idea what a detonated thermonuclear weapon actually looks like, and that tiny, innocent Israel has about 200 of them aimed at any country that believes fascism is an out-dated political philosophy—I bet they even have coordinates set at Yahveh if he too starts to mouth off—Because unmade writers and painters are well-known for crafting nearly endless run-on sentences, I believe that if we don't wake up soon, these life-hat-ing men will pull the pin on a gigundamundus humanity suicide bomb.

There are takers and givers. The bulk of humanity give and take more or less within a relatively microcosmic framework. Each of us is a thoughtless polluter in a global economy, but few openly push for a resurgence of coal-fired power plants knowing the costs to human health. John McCain, nearly dead Arizona Senator[*], runs for President[*] with a rallying cry "Drill, Baby Drill", and millions of working class, non-drilling affiliated spouses, have to listen to dumbed-down taker husbands poison the conversation at the dinner table. Divorce happens eventually—the poor stupid jin-goes never come to the realization that their young wives agreed to marry them precisely because they did not have political opinions. Love begot marriage, and marriage dissolved when love was not good enough for the taker in the family.

I made four paintings in four days. And the week isn't even over yet. I also cleaned the house, did some laundry, cooked all the meals, updated my website, lots of other little things that keep life moving in an orderly manner. In microcosm, I am more of a giver than a taker.

I believe 90% of the people I know and remain liking fall at points on the giving plane. But on a national level, dream statistics don't look so good, even though I suspect it's still a sound major-ity. So, hooray for those of us who would not threaten humanity with either fast or slow annihilation because we want to continue to give on this small planet we all share.

Israel is a theocracy-republic with nuclear weapons headed by a psychopath. Iran is a theocracy republic that would prob-ably like a nuclear weapon or two because their "leaders" are also psychopaths. The United States doesn't know who or what it represents anymore, pretends openly a kind of twisted Billy

Graham-like national religion, has a couple thousand hydrogen bombs, and a spoiled rotten, child psychopath President* who tweets information like a teenager drops endless selfies into the sewer of cyberspace. All of these nation's peoples are represented, rather, controlled, by takers who also happen to be very powerful psychopaths. They are not religious men of peace. Each one in their position is the human opposite of a Martin Luther King. Not courageous, not brave, not admirable in any conceivable way that we measure these virtues by. Likewise, none of them will ever be a you or a me. However, we are all potentially them—that is self-serving, bottom-feeding takers of life.

Bad systems beget bad leaders and bad people.

Good people need to break these systems as quickly as possible. I did my part. So far this week I gave four paintings to the world and completed several necessary household chores. I also said nice things to my family, stayed clear of unsolvable argument, dreamed a bright future for my daughters, and figuratively choked to death the political psychopaths of power.

Your turn. And pass it on.

Within one of my mind's many compartments, I have parked an old tin think tank. I shall climb into it today to sort out some political or cultural confusion, yet also see if I can word strike enough phony politicos to make a collateral damage difference before Armageddon.

Probably not though. Retaliatory strikes are inevitable and possessing very accurate weapons from the arrogant illusion arsenal. Also, my think tank is made of tin, which means that tomorrow, maybe even in an hour, I will have ejected myself with a bouquet of flowers and land at a warm mind beach for some sunrise Tai chi. I am a painter and writer, neither a careerist nor a fanatic. I also prefer guerilla resistance fighting to open confrontation. My enemies desire mechanical murders made from the sky, and prefer to coax little boys and girls out of high school to press the buttons for them.

My political enemies are true and lasting cowards, in it for the long haul. Presently they remain on the right side of the law, holding positions of fantastical power and influence. A U.S. Congressman* claims to represent over 650,000 people. This is an insane claim for certainly 650,000 human beings did not vote for him or her, neither human children nor half the grandmothers and grandfathers disenfranchised at a Medicaid nursing home. The rest of mammalia and all sentient life down our anthropomorphic scale of importance were completely ignored on election day.

So, 99.999% of life is not represented by the one creature alive who literally holds single vote dominion over all of life. One poorly researched "Yay" on the House floor and poof! Everything is dead, even the trees and the Congressman's* own precious loved ones.

To counter and check this heavy cloud atmosphere of ignorance and confusion we elect political representatives to tax us, both figuratively and literally. They start out with some good old-fashioned, clerical government work, but eventually without fail, take frequent, extended excursions into the cultural control arena. The spiritual religious leaders gave up on this approach by Y2K and just agree to whatever the government decrees, except in the viciously fundamental hot spots of Alabama, Israel and Pakistan, where many of their religious representatives want nothing but to smite everything, and then themselves expire into the loving arms of a violently twisted and disgusting god.

To add insult we group-think the very existence of our modern media into the form of an all-knowing bullhorn, even though nearly every single executive, journalist, and even possibly, newsroom custodian, has graduated from a privileged class of über-consumer type A non-individuals. Those people who willingly afford not only the smart phone, but its 2-year contract as well. FOX®, MSNBC®, CNN®, NPR®, ABC® have done nothing in my lifetime besides disrupt, divide and confuse Americans to exasperation.

Likewise, *The New York Times*® only publishes the tragedy, culture and politics of U.S. government interest. And its sister publication, *The Washington Post*®, is owned (therefore controlled) by a delivery boy billionaire (Jeff Bezos), and Americans continue to naively believe in a one, true political world crafted by the propaganda machine, with rank and file set at mouthing perpetual replay.

Talk radio, the NRA®, and Fox News® have fashioned my own father into a gentle bigot. Political correctness, NPR®, and CNN® have turned so many of my friends, family, and myself into equal intellectual dwarfs, and also downright scaredy-cats to power. Some who actually believe that two spoiled rotten human beings should not only run for President®, but actually get somebody's vote. I had a friend express on New Year's Eve about the existence of a protest vote that had ruined his hopeful outcome for the 2016 election. Do you want to know how disconnected I am from my friend's, and also my own (and what I thought were deep set) principles? And how crazy this makes me feel politically? I asked my voting age daughter to tell me who to vote for, because it is her generation that must suffer the horrible choices made today.

She (and I) chose the only candidate who had actually signed her name to the death warrants of a million innocent human babies, and also trillions of other living species like insects and water weeds. The other three were clean. We (the pacifists) voted for the killer.

Contrary to the endless stream of hollow propaganda, there has never been an American spirit. We are a nation of dumbed-down descendants of immigrants, some of the latter who voluntarily arrived, and others who were chained, whipped and bludgeoned onto a ship for a once in a lifetime pleasure trip into Hell.

The American reality is that we are degenerate. Well-caloried and degenerate. That is, we are kept alive and sick, both mentally and physically, for a long life and amount to nothing much besides sentiment memories to our progeny. There are real heroes. Not one of them is in the government nor its military. I do not thank them for their service. If it was service they would do it for free. If it was service, Boeing Inc. would be out of business, and every man Pullman cars would own the new style. If it was service, some children wouldn't be chosen over other children for the luck to keep their vital organs on the working side of their skins.

And yet I participated in a bad system (the general election) even though it continues to perpetuate all the atrocity, human and environmental, that I see happening in the world. Therefore I, as is the majority of Americans, am spiritless, and also a bit cowardly, and unbrave-like. We will do nothing ourselves, but rather vote for rotten human beings until the end of our time.

If you seek real human heroes to counter the onslaught of these faux-brave, state-sponsored Navy® children who suddenly get lauded just because they ordered a whopper on a floating circus aircraft carrier, or, those like my Congressman®, who repeats the phrase "boots on the ground" until no one, not even his own wife, knows what the Hell he is talking about, then read some personal accounts of the civil rights struggles of the past and today. I like the ones from mid-twentieth century or thereabouts, when one could witness the same head get cracked open at nearly the same time, from three different TV channels. And then, to see the victims get up and do it again, and again, in the face of total American bigotry and patriotic correctness— Ho boy! There might not have been an American spirit, but there certainly, most definitely was American courage, and it was nowhere that I am comfortable traveling to these days. I think I would have to cross species to find it.

Recently Charles Thomson, quiet painter from north London, posted a link to a review in The Sunday Times, about a painting exhibition at Saatchi Gallery, a millionaire's mansion of speculative art stuff. I wish I could find it so you could imagine yourself a painter being reviewed by Waldemar Januszcak, the crafty, narcissistic, professional art critic and misanthrope. And, you might feel the pain empathetically, as I did, for other painters an ocean away, and cringe at the flippant arrogance of this poser aiming to please his non-creative betters (the Times editors) during their morning pastries and tea.

I refuse to sully my good taste and break down any critic's article into an argument. Waldemar Januszczak is just another critic who does not make art. A well-oiled bearing in the propaganda machine, to help the sickly skepticism of bloated westerners continue to run like clockwork. Waldemar looks at art, like any person does, and writes about it cruelly for a paycheck.

I won't counter his subjectivity with my own, however, I will make the effort to relegate his type A vanity to the most feared and dangerous monster lair in any creative person's make-believe world.

What does Waldemar do for a career? He writes about other people's creativity and path to self-realization. In his most recent content rant for a newspaper seeking print ads from any prostituting organization that pays, he mocked the career choice of some painters because they did not live up to his highly subjective worldly view of art.

Strike one.

He searched for confirmation of his opinion at Saatchi Gallery, sent by a newspaper editorial board of non-painting millionaires to critique the aesthetic choices of a non-painting art collecting millionaire, Charles Saatchi.

Strike two.

And finally (although I wish several more strikes were allowed in this game), Waldemar's mum and dad raised him to be a sadist.

Strike three.

A few rhetorical questions to follow, all with the answer of "no".

Can a non-painting person ever catch even a chance glimpse into the creative impulses and results of a stranger who paints? Does the latter work a lifetime seeking opinion from strangers whom he or she does not like or love? Can posers like Waldemar reach the freedom of self liberation that so many humble and sensitive human beings on earth strive for? And finally, will an unhappy art critic love art enough to discontinue a professional life spent in mockery of those who seek freedom through art?

Waldemar is an adult counterpart of the six-year-old child who bullied me in the schoolyard. Every day, Brad Davies would find me before the bell rang, to declare it time for my morning punch. Brad was big and scary. I don't think he had any boxing training— just another nasty, spoiled child set up against a kid who appeared weaker because he knew how to be kind. I just wanted to get it over with. After keeling over, I felt freed to finish the day any way I liked. Brad was just a nuisance, like a bath or bowel movement, to whatever private adventures my 6 year old passion would seek.

I should mention that because of Brad, and the many other bullies to follow, I became a staunch protector and champion of the underdog. Reading Waldemar's frightened distrust of painters and especially his wrong knowledge of their painting processes, just turned my visceral reactionary nodules up to high and hot red.

I wish instead of outright mocking their works of art, he congratulated the artists awarded an exhibition at Saatchi Gallery. They finally, after all these years, got their shot at dishwasher salary success. Would not the Times' subscribers have been better served if Waldemar championed the lucky painter's wonderful breakthroughs—an especially rare occurrence in an art world grossly distorted by an upper echelon of frauds (i.e. corporate billionaires)? As a learned art critic, surely he must understand the humiliation, both public and private, that is daily suffered by human beings who "put themselves out there"? Waldemar would get this, right? I mean, with his extensive training in art history, he at least got a B in Private Struggle 101, yes?

Waldemar Januszczak is a non-creative bully, a sadist, like little Brad Davies. I picture him as a brother in some college fraternity practically hazing to death hopeful initiates. In art history class he snickers to his dumb buddies during the lecture on van Gogh. "What a loser!" he says. I suspect, had he an art critic's freelance opportunity in 1880, Waldemar would have published a loaded pistol of criticism about van Gogh, calling out the poor man to quit painting and avoid all that unnecessary suffering.

My wife and I discussed Waldemar's article. She didn't want me to be too hard on him. She's a very pretty woman, and as a young girl did not suffer a daily Brad Davies' gut punch. Nor has she has ever been insulted in a workaday world of mutual politeness. I have to educate her on the manner of a cruel world and those art critics who seek to undo much that healthy expression has to offer, in order to protect their own professional relevance.

I have very strong opinions, but unlike Waldemar, I am not a public twit. And, I can admit to all and sundry that I am an artist who doesn't even like art very much. Likewise, as an artist I can promise you, and I'll stake my "career" success on it, that Waldemar, not only does not like art, but he is determined to punch it in the gut until it cries. His betters, who sell everything from recycled toenail clippers, to highly absorbent paper towels, would not have it any other way. They have an agenda. A world of artists would make for absolutely rotten consumers of the trite and inane. Millionaires of no creativity, and their viable army of sycophant soldiers like Waldemar, subsist to make creative people question their own powers of creation. They keep good people guessing while the sad people buy more useless crap to make the dumb millionaires even richer. Owners of The Sunday Times not excluded.

It will end someday when masses of humanity cease to put faith into the media trolls of planet earth. Top down media is dying. The people have gotten smart to the old time censoring of realities. Likewise a million trolls die every second on the Internet. For Waldemar to remain relevant, he'll have to paint a picture someday and have it hang in a parlor at a party, or uploaded and criticized in cyberspace. Like the Stuckists do every day. Meanwhile he remains an art gossip, anyone's mother or brother, with a subjective opinion about none of his business.

Lastly, during that same conversation, my wife agreed that I would continue to paint, even if I remained a dishwasher sharing the rent with other dishwashers for a flat on skid row. Every day, day after day, I would practice my art. To know if Waldemar can be a valuable tool to criticize artists who paint for reasons other than getting paid, we should ask if he would continue his career if nobody gave him two pence of a shit.

Ha! The sadist without encouragement. Brad Davies ran home and cried into his pillow.

Artists of earth know very well that Waldemar is a coward. He would know it too if he dared some day to make his own oeuvre of paintings and show them to his friends and some strangers. I shall take my wife's advice, and be nice. May the art critic live a long, satisfied, myopic life, and die alone and soon forgotten even by his grandchildren. To the Saatchi painters he criticized for receiving career changing attention on a late autumn day, I give you all the following advice and encouragement:

Just keep painting. Because even if you're a total ass like Waldemar Januszczak, at least the progeny of your line will remember you for as long as it takes plastic or oil to disintegrate.

¡Viva la Stuckism!

Democrans and Rebublicrats restrict reality to what they read in the newspapers.

Recently I painted a bear atop the Burlington Electric Department up in Vermont, where it is cold, like Siberia. This huge Russian bear empties an old honey jug of hydrochloric acid all over the electric grid in order to infiltrate American homes with fake news and pro Donald Trump propaganda. He is also a consummate hypnotist and can manipulate any mind away from reason and rationale into a devoted post neo-con loving, Confederate flag waving, Rudy Giuliani, gaudily over-dressed in endangered animal skins.

This most recent fake news story came from the powerhouse propaganda corporation, The Washington Post®. Coupled with the almost declassified unverified intelligence report on election Facebook ads by Russia, it had a huge impact on worldwide media opinion and turned many in my nation, (who by virtue of what I have learned through social psychological research, were already very North Korea lite and vulnerable to government propaganda), into Facebook® political hacks. Even some of my more sensitive Facebook® friends couldn't leave it alone. The sky is falling! The sky is falling! Chicken Littles with very little, or at best, woefully forgotten historical education. It seems the only political triumph sought is the removal, by impeachment or volunteer abdication, of the most recent President®-elect. No ideologies are being expressed. No anti-war protest, or reminders of rapid environmental deterioration. All of the bad in the world, many of these Facebook®ers decree, can only be fixed by the removal of this one man and his sinister lair of cabinet appointees. He is the sole road block to every potential good mankind can promote or achieve. If we rise up collectively to Facebook® and Twitter® troll him day and night, then surely we can oust this monster from power, and then all will be right with the world. Our government will cease to be the number one arms dealer to Earth, Inc. The U.S. will immediately sever all connections with insane states of insanity like Saudi Arabia and Israel, and we shall get back to the clear-minded and reasonable policies of Barack Obama, and continue where his administration left off, pushing for a trillion dollar nuclear upgrade, bombing the be-Jesus out of poor oil path nations, charging the poor for health insurance, watching helplessly while BP® or its equivalent, churns another Gulf of Mexico into a thick crude oil shake.

I am witnessing people use social media to right the world order, when they have never known a right world order, nor are even able to dream of one unless their political enemies are defeated. They cannot or rather, will not do it themselves. That kind of thinking is crazy, forgetting all the while that both Hitler and Gandhi were small, rather insignificant themselves at one time.

If Facebook® is to work as a tool for positive change, it needs to replace it's "Like" thumb with a meet-up link. That is, if you like Jimmy's post about a beer he drank in Harvard Square, you can arrange for a place to connect with Jimmy (perhaps a pub) and discuss the virtues of that beer and maybe more of its kind. Or, if Jimmy is a staunch, flag-waving Democran or Republicrat, you can forgo the cute little thumb's up, or the deafening silence of the dreaded no-thumb disapproval, or worse yet, the tell-tale nonplussed reaction expressed in comment mocking of your politics, and actually spend an hour or two peacefully assembling with others of like-hope in Jimmy's house, if he ever can let go of his many internal fears, and actually invite you over sometime. Nope. Let us Facebook® our politics instead. That is how we can tell revolution is just around the corner. Or, wait a second—check out this adorable puppy licking that parrot's eyeball!

I believe this to be the more likely scenario: Facebook® will remain just a cyber hangout for some very nice people, but also quite a few impotent trolls as well, discussing the vices and much less often, the virtues, of each other's ranky-dank under bridge hideout.

I would like to finish up with a popular story out of the annals of social psychology research describing the "Bystander Effect".

In 1964, a young woman named Catherine Genovese was raped and killed in two separate attacks in Queens, N.Y. After investigation police noted that 38 people had either witnessed the violence or heard Genovese scream, but at no time did anyone make an effort to scare off the attacker, and just one woman called the police. There are many situations like this happening every day. They used to call it cowardice before PC made everyone equally special so long as they possessed a router in their home.

Facebook® is by and far the greatest promoter of the bystander effect. And it works a kind of magic on our brain's sensitive clan approval cortex. Nobody does anything of substance anymore. Or, at least it appears that way. The completion of a book to be published is liked as well as the latest video of a cat stuffing itself into a flower vase. This summer, thanks to Facebook Live®, I even got to witness with my own eyes an actual murder on the side of the road. I didn't like it one bit. I left my angry face emoticon for all and sundry to contemplate. I was so mad. I went into the kitchen and made myself a sandwich.

Zuckerberg bets we don't do a damn thing with our minds and bodies besides twiddle our thumbs and continue to debate news stories we read or see on TV. I think he likes it when some nonconformist fool tips the moderate scales just a wee little bit with a thought expressed about everlasting peace. You should see the bystanders rise up and—comment like the world is about to end. But then Jeopardy is on at 7:00 PM, and the social media victim probably deserved exactly what she got anyway.

Facebook® is a place for mind and do rot.

One last quote, and then Facebook® is that embarrassing coffee table fluff book I hide away when guests stop by.

*I have named the destroyers of nations: comfort, plenty, and security out of which grow a bored and slothful cynicism, in which rebellion against the world as it is, and myself as I am, are submerged in listless self-satisfaction.*

—John Steinbeck (famous non-Facebook®er)

Here is my marker for citizen non-compliance:
A glass of water and a hot shower in Flint, Michigan.

Any takers? And I don't mean just one sip of one glass of water, like our outgoing President® took a couple springs back. I'm talkin' a USDA 8 cups a day, day after day guzzle, and a few hot caustic showers a week to prove that, yes, our government has ample power and wealth to make municipal plumbing improvements in Flint.

The United States and its state of Michigan are derelict. When governments are consistently derelict in duties to the people, they are unreliable, and unreliable in many cases equates to weak. Therefore, in reality, the superpowers seated in Washington and Lansing are rather ineffective and lame. I don't know about you, but I tolerate them like little faraway cousins at a family reunion. They're a pain in the arse when bouncing around me, but not of much importance in my every day life. In fact, not important at all.

And yet, the truly great American activist Michael Moore (and I mean this with high respect) is busying himself these days trying his darnedest to oust a President-elect® with Twitter®, or making movies for profit, or whatever the hell he does with all that freakin' money besides release it and revolt! He keeps using the old rusty master's tools long after Boeing® raided the golden work shed to make slick homicide bombs for slimy old prostates to play drop on a family with. Michael, with all his people power and righteous influence, would better serve America if he planted his organization right down in central Flint, made daily broadcasts from there, practically non-stop, like a Jerry Lewis Telethon, until some of that delicious mafia arms dealing money is turned over to the people of that desperate city, at least so much so that by next Christmas kids can drink a god damn glass of water and remember how to multiply at the same time.

Weak and ineffective government.

I read yesterday that Barack Obama's progressive legacy among sending his kids to private school, keeping the Guantanamo Bay torture complex open 24-7, and deporting 2.5 million immigrants back to from where they came, also included an average of three bombs dropped every hour for eight years on tan and tanner people in other parts of the world who Americans never care about until they're told to care about them. Which means, bomb them. Not to mention the BP oil disaster—oops! Just a little leak. 11 people dead. Billions of Gulf of Mexico things dead—What an unfortunate accident, and not one executive put on trial. But such a nasty fine! And this morning's stock futures look to be on the rise...

Go Tar Sands!

Ineffective government.

I actually believe Trump's inauguration will usher in some positive, progressive accomplishment. All these angry pretend liberals will roll over the pretend conservatives with an unmitigated onslaught of tweets, releasing a massive silent war wave of he-said, she-saids. And by this time next year there will be just 800 homicides in Chicago. Not too bad. Actually, pretty darn good for Twitter®, or MSNBC®, or Fox News®, or where ever you plan to be Michael Moore, instead of in Flint, where real suffering is happening right now. All you're doing today is riling up comfortable jackasses like me to be angry at something none of us has been able to change since money was invented. This finger-pointing game has made you quite a wealthy man. Stop reaching everywhere. Pick a battle and remain until the fat lady gets offed by some real nifty Boeing-designed and created metallic drone spray.

I wish my friends and Michael Moore would get over this football game called Presidential politics. I wish they could judge our government how our government and its people judged the fascists of Italy and Germany during the late Depression just prior to World War II. I truly wish they could understand how just one, small by comparison, WMD invention of our industrial war designers gets displayed before the people on the wrong side of its manufacture. Just a little imagination please!

Americans are just so damn arrogant, blind, and numb-dumb. If you don't like what you get for what you give, stop giving. Divorce these crooks in Washington. You will never-ever vote them out. Nazi Germany when victorious, had a lot of Germans eating good German bread and drinking good German beer. Americans see no correlation because the atomic bomb was invented, and then the military industrial complex got excited. The MIC meant to the people of the world outside of the U.S. that, had no atomic weapons been created, and these U.S. governments still carried on in the cutting up and control of masses of peoples all over the globe year after year, then arrogant America would have been overrun a long time ago, invaded and conquered, before the Beatles® even, and the rest of the British invasion. Proliferation of military might is the only reason we are still an intact nation. If Nazis had 2000 nuclear weapons for 70 years after World War II, then Volkswagen® would be top automaker even if it admitted to all and sundry that its cars were made out of Swiss cheese. Swiss *people cheese*.

My God, these jokers created a department with the word "Homeland" in it, and not one of us, even the most astute, jumped a little recognition jump of "Holy shit, they're insane!"

That is impressive control! And from a weak and ineffective government.

Wake up Michael Moore. Help create a true resistance at a real place and time. Lay your money down, and go back to Flint. Let's turn this broken sewer government into capable Hoover Dam plumbers once again.

I want Medicare for all. I want this, and can have it because I do not want another aircraft carrier with a Taco Bell® catering subsidized careers to high school underachievers. Drones are cheaper and can pick off innocent people, or cumbersome dictators thousands of miles away. My government tests them out of Syracuse, N.Y. Some pimply little brat from X-box® school pretends suburbs like Mattydale and Liverpool are hostile insurgent camps and he aims its sights on a Syracuse school bus from an air-conditioned cubicle in Reno, Nevada. Drones are very affordable as they are immoral, however, as a replacement to the Lockheed Martin® and Boeing® dinosaurs, they potentially free up billions of dollars for prenatal care to expectant mothers, and a college education promised to their newborns approximately 18 years after delivery.

I know that the national treasury can afford these things because I can find out the cost of an obsolete fighter jet online. So can you. During my upcoming 2018 independent run for New York's 24th district Congressional seat, I will do my best to refrain from spouting statistics to back up an argument. Americans pay a federal tax, the numbers add up to a very large sum, and from that sum funds are distributed by Congress® back to government and its many bureaucratic functions. Citing the amount we pay now in federal tax, and foregoing obsolete 20th century investment in aircraft carriers and airbases in Afghanistan and Okinawa, I know our nation can afford health care for all, make significant payments on the national debt, and offer top notch education to our children.

Here are some campaign promises. I can offer nothing more or less. I will not debate another candidate. I will not speak of qualifications, nor defend my past. The constitution has already qualified me. I am over 25. I have been a citizen of the United States and lived in New York State for 50 years, and my children love me. That is enough.

1. I will serve only one term.

2. I will take the salary for the two years I am representative, and donate half to a one time meritorious scholarship opportunity for two high school students in my district.

3. I will not take a pension in any form (see #1).

4. I will hire only one staff secretary if allowed by rules of Congress°.

5. I will only vote on bills that I am able to read in full, given the time allotted to read them. I will only vote in a manner ascribed by the United States Constitution°. That is, read it yourself. If you like it enough to vote for me, then please do.

6. While Congress-person, I will make no appearances in public outside of my offices, the steps of U.S. Congress°, or on my way to the mailbox.

7. I will not have any contact with lobbyists. Only individual constituents representing themselves or local non-profits.

8. I will support the ratification initiation of several amendments to the Constitution° if circulating Congress° while I am serving my one and only term.

9. I will not vote on any social or cultural issue, yet openly advocate and educate on the amendment process. So, if you love or hate my stance on social issues, please take note that throughout my term I will abide only by the precepts set forth on this issues page.

Finally, and this may come as a surprise to both established parties, I very much intend to win, or lose, depending on how seriously I am taken. Still, I believe if given a sober third choice advocating passionate political reason, that only an ignoramus would cast a vote for a same ole republicrat, or same ole democran, knowing what he or she has come to know about our failing institution of federal government.

I think I have a pretty good chance.

Or not.

I have been reading over my father's mini-autobiography this week with many questions about the validity of his observations. He is very nostalgic throughout, yearning for a past that he swears by all accounts truly happened. And I believe his memory, though question his interpretations of it. Contrary to his purer thoughts on matrimony, women did get pregnant out of wedlock in 1961. The term "shotgun wedding" was not invented by my generation, nor by millennials downloading the next fab app that will drive them to interestingness come hell or cool board game. And his assumptions about how happy women were to aspire to home economics for a god damn lifetime while their husbands flirted with secretaries, hunted slow pheasants and spouted 5th grade newspaper opinions, is downright insulting to millions and billions of daughters we raise today to be free of misogynist child-men who only desire their wives as lifelong pillowcases. My Dad does admit throughout that the old always rebel against the younger generation (rather than the other way around), and I find that introspective to an honorable degree. However, the political labeling of his family while growing up in the 40's and 50's is not only questionable, but provides keen insight into today's mass delusion.

My Dad claims in all seriousness that his dad (my grandfather Ronald) was an Eisenhower Republican*, leaning politically toward a new hopeful age of liberty. After WWII, Grandpa Ronald raised his two boys (with the buffer of a completely satisfied woman whose brain was second in command to the high man brain in the family), to be self-sufficient, like he, in every possible endeavor. Being Depression era children themselves, in spring, Grandpa Ronald planted an acre vegetable garden in a residential neighborhood of peers who would rather acquire all produce magically at the new supermarkets, and Grandma Evelyn stocked a basement full of canned preserves in the autumn. They pinched pennies, darned socks, and ate potatoes, while saving an enormous amount of money in their lifetime. Enough to provide all five grandchildren with an undergraduate education, and relative comfort to my dear grandmother who outlived Grandpa Ronald by 22 years.

But here is the rub, and it's eerily Mao Zedong-ish—

Grandpa Ronald lived his entire adult life dependent on socialism. Sure, he could call himself whatever he wanted—an Eisenhower Republican*, lover of freedom, citizen-champion of man's liberation from tyranny, potato farmer—We can pretend whatever we want to be. But whichever way you look at it, as it pertained to how he acquired a regular income, Grandpa Ronald was a practicing socialist. Just out of engineering school at Cornell in 1936, he took a job working in the shipyards of the U.S. Navy. From 1941-1945, was cut a paycheck by the U.S. Army working as a field lieutenant under General George Patton, and for the rest of his life he worked as an engineer and planner for the New York State Highway Department. Every job he had out of college was subsidized by federal and state taxpayers. That is macro and microeconomic socialism in a nutshell. Every seed packet-purchased pea my Dad ate as a boy was provided to him by his neighbors, whether they wanted to help, or not. Even good ole Eisenhower, the mass killer turned President*, got paid by the good graces of national neighbors. Socialist!

Quite a profound realization, in a political sense. Since I am running for Congress in 2018, I need to account for my income, which comes solely from my wife's hard work outside the home. She is employed by the State of New York, therefore all we have accumulated in material treasure, the roof over our heads, the food on our plates, and also the fuel to our furnace, has been subsidized by the good people of New York State. I want to thank you all for this socialism. Our family depends on you.

I have a bosom buddy who works as a corrections officer for the New York State prison authority. Lately he's been leaning right in his politics. Nope. Unless he quits by this afternoon, he is also a socialist pinko, and a hypocrite to boot.

John Katko, who I believe I'll be running against for office in

2018, is also so very, very socialist. It cost a heap of taxpayer money to supply his salary and pension, and likewise to put all those feet into army "boots on the ground", one of his favorite public expressions.

And all you good soldiers at Fort Drum, I have to say, are also tried and true socialists. You could join a non-profit militia if finding the need to keep your politics clean, however, I don't think meals will be as regular, and you might accidentally hurt innocent people.

The janitors and groundskeepers of local schools, and county and state institutions all over my district, some fireman, every police man or woman, my assemblyman and state senator—all are rank and file socialists!

And that is just how they depend on their living. Like me, they could not pretend their present and future politics without the blessing of a populace that has chosen to shelter, heat, feed, and clothe them for a lifetime.

So, as your future congress person, I would now like to declare a first issue of mine (and I hope yours too!): I admit that I am a reluctant socialist who would advocate to allocate the money out of the U.S. Treasury into securing dignity in old age to our fathers and mothers. Medicaid for all who need it, and the end of for profit nursing care.

Money to dignity, not demagoguery!

Throop for Congress 2018!

Like communism, capitalism weighs very little on the U.S. political scale. On the micro-economic level, my existence as a painter has been influenced mostly by the anti-capitalism that exists on every level of government. I began my working life and private passion as a cook and aspiring chef in a local restaurant. In a truly capitalistic environment, I would have continued a career in the culinary arts/service industry straight through to retirement. The natural progression of my talent through practice, the skills and knowledge gained, set me on a course to acquiring my own restaurant and competing with other food industry entrepreneurs on a local level. A true capitalism would have offered no barriers beyond my abilities to taking the small risk of maintaining a 33% and under food cost, and practicing good kitchen habits to prevent food born disease to my customers. I would have begun serving sandwiches and hot soups to passersby on days off out in the front yard of the first apartment I rented after college. I would save my profits, and expand my business at every opportunity to one day afford a building to rent that had decent plumbing and electricity.

I was a very good cook once—self-taught, like all successful art must be, with true dedication in learning and practice. Before the Internet, I visited the library often to take out cookbooks, dreamed preparations at night for restaurant specials the next day, and at the time, also had a dabbler's interest in Zen Buddhism, easily weaving the latter into the story of the cook's life I was writing.

However, because of existing political philosophies used in practice, the risks to restaurant entrepreneurship were too great to delve into without an exorbitant upfront investment provided by a bank or wealthy investor. A pretend capitalism of and by the rich to steer the poor away from self-sufficiency.

America's anti-capitalism, as it exists towards the lower financial classes, prevented a start-up that could have developed into a family-supporting success. There were and are just too many barriers to private investment in the food industry. The most obvious are local codes set up to create commercial zoning, which inflates commercial rents and realty to points out of reach for most start-ups. So, at an earlier age, I was prevented by non-capitalistic codes for a fair shot at failure or success. My bootstraps didn't even get the chance to be laced, let alone pulled up.

So incremental risks I could have made were denied by the political and economic powers in place, which are never true capitalism, more than it is a business of the rich for the more well-off socialists, at least as it pertains to local economies today.

Therefore, my career story lies on a path of least resistance. Paints, word processing software, and an Internet connection are affordable, whereas an investment in a commercial district restaurant enterprise is not. Pretend capitalists would say that I was just avoiding risk. A $200,000.00 loan to a man who has $3,000.00 saved and a self-taught plan to serve French sauces to the community is a ludicrous risk which no pretend capitalist would ever take. The poor cook would be laughed out of any bank in the land. True risk begins on a fair playing field, and rewards those who outshine competition over time. I am probably not the best painter and writer in my county. But I was one of the best potential restauranteurs. Today the restaurants in my community, save a couple family treasures (begun in the mid-20th century) are downright horrible. Yet even where the family restaurants shine (service and acceptable ambiance), the food is mostly average to bad.

Which leads to another issue to consider for my independent run for New York's 24th district congressional seat...

Advocate to our state government a capitalism-socialism for all new business. Any one should be able to start a passion money-maker, yet must be required to follow all local, state and federal health, safety, and environmental guidelines, not pertaining to physical existence zoning. Neighborhood mom and pop grocery stores, doctor and dentist offices, plumbers, electricians, schools, and of course, restaurants, all developing and thriving in residential neighborhoods.

The crowding of retail and restaurant chains like Walmart® and McDonalds® is not born from a rugged individualistic kind of capitalism—they are put into place by outside oligarchal pathogens infecting local communities. Last Saturday I got into a discussion with a woman at the art association about a debate going on in the small village where she resides. There is a faction of towns-people protesting the arrival of a new Dollar General® dollar store franchise. She claims that the poor need it, and the rich don't want it for all of its unsightliness. (It shows the town's poor acting poor). I told her that if the village would allow for residential businesses to be created, then even the poor could take their chances at local financial autonomy by going into business, and at the same time voice their own shunning of the big box China crap house chains popping up all over the U.S., making a profit on despair. Both her and I agreed on the business model—big chain moves in, makes a ten-year long profit on an initial 1/4 million dollar investment (oftentimes tax-free for ten years by local government looking to wage-slave their constituents), and the town gets cheap, mostly unnecessary goods for a decade and then Dollar General® leaves town, leaving an ugly (and empty) cement box.

I want to change this paradigm by nationally advocating for a more rugged (and safely regulated) localism. A true capitalism-socialism blend for the middle class and poor that could make for closer, more socially responsible communities—responsible to each other as cohabitating human beings.

With unexpected success in the 2018 election, I may get the chance someday to serve sandwiches and soups out of my garage.

Or at least paintings of them anyway.

News this morning says that a big penis bomb was dropped
on the subterranean compound in Afghanistan killing 36 ISIS
fighters. All bad guys according to the Pentagram, I mean *Pentagon*, upside-down crucifix, Hellslayer, motherkillers... Whatever
the name for "Satan Central" is these days. So I get low some
mornings down in the basement studio, knowing that, with a dead
Constitution, we are all just a broken people without a country.
And I paint emotionally.

The Pentagon thought a million Vietnamese were all "bad guys".
A million Iraqis too. 300 million dollars (cost of exploding penis)
to kill 36 repressed suicide bombers, and our heavily guarded and
cowardly sheltered, eye-brow-cured "leader" declares it a success.
And yet, the ISIS gang can achieve equal success, and more by
murdering innocents at an airport, or shopping mall, or public
park—wherever the heck they want to. And all they need for it is
some wires, TNT, an electrician, and of course a man or woman
whose child was killed by the Pentagram, I mean, Pentagon, no, I
mean upside-down crucifix, Hellslayer, killer of mothers...

My God, this broken war-mongering state has made so many
psychologically sick persons that it wouldn't be difficult to recruit
a few, and for a million bucks a pop, strap some explosives to their
bodies and drop them from airplanes onto any heavily ISIS'd
desert military compound, or, tit for tat, an ISIS airport (Oh wait,
they don't have any of those), shopping mall (none of those either),
or public park (nope, zippy, nada). There are many American
life failures who might offer up their bodies for a cool mil to be
collected by loved ones after a successful mission. And it would

simultaneously free up millions for home improvement. Infra-structure, housing, health care, you name it!

Nope. The corporito mafia wouldn't get its cut.

Anyway, Happy Easter! In 2004, during the recent memory insanity of constitutionally illegal Iraq war, I wrote the following open letter and mailed 40 copies to all the religious houses in my city and countryside. Hummers were delivering their broken, psychotic families to church, while the paid-for military was spreading disease all over the globe. It was time to scold the scared little preacher lambs. They weren't doing their Jesus job. Cost me 40 stamps and I never got one reply.

### An Open Letter to My Local Messengers of the Gospel to be Read Aloud This Easter Sunday

Earlier today I heard over my car radio that a mosque in Fallu-jah, Iraq had been struck by three U.S. missiles. A Mosque in Iraq. Missiles. In 1938 rocks were thrown at Jews and their windows. *The Night of Broken Glass*. Today, April 8, 2004, forty Iraqis were blown to pieces by your governemnt. A sacred house. A holy shrine. Today I believe this mosque to be the holiest place on earth. Jesus was one of those children inside, crouching, holding his tiny ears while your governemt assassins melted him.

This Easter Jesus will die for Iraqi children. Why should he even bother with the Americans? Our children are not in need of any god or its savior. Our children have been orphaned by the holy spirit.

So now you know what has happened, and what will you do about it? Myself? I stuck my head out the car window and screamed a thousand curses on mankind. With all my vocal might I shouted out hate until I nearly passed out with rage. If war is crazy, then a church that is silent about war is criminally insane. Criminal to Jesus Christ. To men, to birds of the air and beasts of the land and of the sea. A mosque is burning and children are screaming for their mothers and fathers. Grief is destroying the families of Iraq and I must do my part to block your false Easter joy with cries of their suffering.

I am tired of crying my heart out to fallow fields, to oblivious trees and squirrels. It is time to confront the men of my village. The truth is that your church is partly responsible for the premeditated murder of human beings. I call on you to end the global murder perpetuated by your silence, your acquiescence, your private tax dollars, and those of the congregation. You have a moral pulpit and therefore a responsibility to God and his flock to right the wrongs of your brothers and sisters.

The children of Afghanistan, Iraq, Palestine... Are you not getting the story correct? Who is David and who is Goliath? If Jesus was walking the streets of Fallujah this morning, where would he run to when all hell broke loose? To the mosque of the holy spirit, or to the Bradley tank? Do I have the New Testament wrong? Have I been away so long that Christianity has warped into a reliable adjunct of the Pentagon? Do you ever wonder why people don't pack full your churches? Do you speak for Jesus or the American emperor? Are you a Pharisee, a mobster, a coward? For God's sake, stop reading Christ as if he were literate! You know as well as me when the gospel was written. You know who wrote it too. A good comparison would be the Indian Parliament in the year 2300 interpreting Ghandi's message for the masses, with uplifting words as well as a massive arsenal of nuclear weapons.

Please, I beg you, the suffering people of Iraq are deserving of good news this Easter. Say something for them if you can claim understanding of anything Jesus. Why so many preachers live the better part of their spiritual lives in Revelations will always be a mystery to me. Maybe fear and impotence play a larger role than I had imagined. Maybe after all, the lot of you just suffer from spiritual envy. You can't deny that those Muslims sure know how to feel! I think regular doses of suffering would make us better believers too, but unfortunately Walmart doesn't carry any of that in stock. In America, Sunday church is only as palatable as the brunch afterwards. The latter is always too cheap for real maple syrup. The former just gyps the spirit.

For Chist's sake, go our into the streets this Easter! At least lead your congregation on a march through the parking lot. Point to the machines that are warming the atmosphere. Help them to understand what it means to not have a habitable planet. For contrary to present Christian representative opinion, global warming is a Jesus problem. Also nuclear weapons, the military budget, the Patriot Act... Jesus, these are all very good Jesus problems. I'm afraid that the real revelation these days is that most of you are so far gone from the teachings of Christ that American Christian spirituality is one of the world's biggest jokes. You are good comedy. Funny like the Morris family in Uganda preaching the gospel to unbelievers. I think that a Ugandan purse-snatcher has more Jesus in him than all the Morris family and their church sponsors combined. Why? Because chances are that that poor sinner has actually suffered.

Americans don't suffer. They weep into their pillows and buy cars. And you, who could possess so much authority in your own house, allow them too many transgressions, even these mass murders of late. Why? For your own security?

For the sake of all God's creatures, risk your jobs this Easter Sunday. Tell the people what they do not want to hear. Give to the Iraqi children who have died for you. Cease negotiations with the emperor. Let the people come to your mosque for reasons of life and death. But first tell the people what they damn well need to hear. That Jesus Christ would not be proud of them. At least no Jesus of my heart would die for these hide-behind-missile child murderers.

The killing must stop now. It is your job to stop it. Make our Jesus proud! Imitate the Christ this Easter.

Marie is my wife. Or, I am her husband. They say possession is 9/10 the law, and to anyone looking, it's obvious that we are close—married to the hilt— bearing all the positive and negative of that attachment vice/virtue the Buddhists claim is soul draining. So, emotionally, we possess each other, for better or worse, like good/bad attachments. We "get it", and flow fairly well together, through good and bad, in concert with fluctuating hormonal balances—her month, my month, hair loss, hair gain... We have nearly mastered the art of cohabitation, and she, whether realizing it or not, is primed and ready for a sweet nirvana, if she ever desires/not desires its potential awakening.

Me, on the other hand, is an anxious mess. The culprit (if I must ascribe blame. And I must because I am not healed) is culture, and the roles it pressures us into, wittingly or unwittingly. Marie is breadwinner. We eat and stay dry and warm because she maintains acceptable work outside the home. A steady job that pays well enough for me to stay home and keep life about us steady and content. I am literally bread-maker—stay-at-home cook and part-time butler, part-time painter, writer, curator. These are the chores separating me from Marie, for we are both very sensitive, full time spouse and parent, and there should be no comparisons made in these departments. I am an okay cook, decent butler, yet would fail the most lenient Emily Post white-glove inspection.

Selective breeding among male Throops carried on fairly well without me for 56,000 years, and then Marie and I came along and upset the stream. Damned it up good and proper, I'd say, for I haven't gone a day in my adult life without some manner of confusion about my place and role(s) in a society that worships nothing but abstractions—namely, money.

To say I am an anxious person would be a gross understatement. I am more like an outwardly successful squirrel, yet unsatisfied with myself in a world of squirrels that covets and adores a mutual abstraction. Squirrels around me who act like squirrels day after day, accumulating nuts, building impressive nests, braving seasons and storms, but underlying every accomplishment is the pressing desire to accumulate the abstraction that will make the squirrel a new squirrel, refined prince or princess in squirrel kingdom. I am infected with the abstraction also, which makes me a constantly dissatisfied squirrel. Let's say this abstraction occupying us squirrels practically night and day is the desire to accumulate human manufactured snow-globes. Many generations ago, some wise and economically trained squirrel scribes thought to create a falling leaf money supply to ease and simplify transactions among squirrels of Squirreldom, however knowing the ubiquitous existence of trees, sought a limited, countable base currency to give an abstract value to something that was readily available in Squirreldom—leaves. Leaf banks opened up practically overnight, followed by upstanding squirrels founding colleges and universities, the development of a million acceptable leaf-paying occupations (none of them nut gathering), and finally a culturally devastating, squirrel-separating atomization.

Anyway, I had a dream last night, my last one about money if hope can help it. I was at Donald Trump's next wedding and the cheapskate expected a gift. 60 dollars is a lot when you can't make that in a month from painting. Marie's brother from D.C. was there with his wife telling her in a false admiring, deeply condescending way, that it was "too cool" that I painted—Oh, but I could see the mockery in his eyes and hear it in the tone of his voice. Shamed again! And not for the last time that night. After the gifts were laid out for all and sundry to see, Trump had my gift, a painting, taken out and thrown in the trash. Marie confided to me that she provided a back-up without my knowledge—a Samsung® tablet for the new bride. I was so mad. I stormed out of the tent and went to sleep on a servant's cot in some nearby dusty garage. The end.

Faith that my marriage is secure, I intend to reach my end beating to death inside me this false god money. Whenever I have deep doubt, (and that is as often as dinner), I will take that negative energy and with it,  push as hard as I can into a positive dream. This money god has got us squirrels absolutely frazzled. All my nuts aren't secure, but I know where to find them. I had no faith in gods. I want no faith in money. I will play my faith at this marriage and focus my dreams on a persistent present moment. I will continue to write and paint erratically, like a squirrel caught both ways in the road, nutless.

www.ingramcontent.com/pod-product-compliance
Lightning Source LLC
Chambersburg PA
CBHW050514290526
45786CB00007B/2567